Little Book of

TASSELS

Danielle Chiel

SALLY MILNER PUBLISHING
(MILNER CRAFT SERIES)

DEDICATION

Dedicated to my two most ardent supporters
Jeremy and Michael Chiel.

First published in 2000 by
Sally Milner Publishing Pty Ltd
PO Box 2104
Bowral NSW 2576
AUSTRALIA

© Danielle Chiel 2000

Design by Anna Warren, Warren Ventures P/L
Editing by Lyneve Rappell
Photography by Sergio Santos

Printed in Hong Kong

National Library of Australia
Cataloguing-in-Publication data:
    Chiel, Danielle
      Little book of tassels

      ISBN 1 86351 260 8.

      1. Tassels. I. Title. (Series : Milner craft series).
    746.27

Disclaimer
The information in this instruction book is presented in good faith. However, no warranty is given, nor results guaranteed, nor is freedom from any patent to be inferred. Since we have no control over the use of information contained in this book, the publisher and the author disclaim liability for untoward results.

Contents

Introduction

This book shows how to make tassels that have a wooden head as their base. These sorts of tassels have served a decorative, yet practical, purpose for many years. They have been used mostly for curtain tie backs and for decorations on chairs. However, now they have become an art form in their own right.

The statement, 'They are beautiful,' is often followed by the question, 'What do I do with them?' If you wish to make a particular tassel, but it does not match your bedroom décor, and your curtains do not need tie backs, it may make a stunning piece of art hanging from the wall of your home.

These tassels have been designed and chosen with simplicity in mind. The techniques are basic and the emphasis is on experimenting with colour, texture and shape. Most of these tassels can be made in a couple of hours, and, as the projects are all clearly explained, you can begin anywhere in the book. It is not necessary to start at the beginning.

The projects have been grouped together to introduce techniques for the different parts of the tassel. The first section demonstrates how to decorate the head, how to change colours as you wrap and how to add a second layer of decoration. These projects have simple skirts and waist decorations. The second group elaborates on the simple skirts by varying length and colour, and adding decorations. Instructions for the delightful ribbon skirts, in this section, introduce a very different look to the tassels. The final group shows how to embellish the waist using ribbons, gathered ruffs and soft tassels. Many of the tassels are striking for their simplicity, others are gorgeously decorative, but they are all worth a try.

Several of these projects have been made using corded thread for wrapping the wooden form and for hanging the tassel. You can make cord using a corder if you have one available, otherwise purchased cord, plaited threads or simple ribbons make beautiful hangings.

The Parts of a Tassel

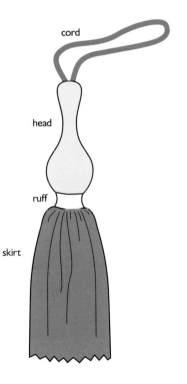

cord

head

ruff

skirt

The parts of a tassel

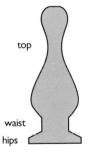

top

waist

hips

The wooden form
The parts of the wooden forms are called the hips (base), the waist, and the top.

Requirements

ALL PROJECTS

- Scissors.

- A wooden tassel form (see Suppliers at the back of this book).

- Glue. Different types of glue are required depending on the type of thread used to cover the head. Spray glue works best with finer threads. The fact that it does not visually stain the thread is a favourable aspect of this glue. However, spray glue does not seem to hold some of the thicker threads, and tacky craft glue is used in these instances.

- Threads to cover the wooden form for the cord and/or the waist (listed with each project). Prepare the thread for wrapping around the wooden head by unwinding the skein and wrapping it around the back of a chair. This will help to stop the thread from tangling.

- Ribbons for the cord and/or the waist (listed with each project).

- Material for the skirt—either ready made commercial fringing or ribbons (details with each project).

- Needle and thread. These are used to secure the skirt and waist covering.

- Thin wire. This is used to pull the cord through the hole in the centre of the wooden form and attach it so that it doesn't fall out.

MAKING YOUR OWN CORD

- A corder (see Cord for directions). If you can't get hold of a corder, plaiting makes an excellent multicoloured cord, and simple twists make good one or two coloured cords.

- Dental floss. This is used to secure the threads at the ends of the cord.

WHEN USING SPRAY GLUE

- Plastic wrap (to cover the base of the wooden form if using spray glue).

- A rubber glove. It is used for a rather practical purpose—so that glue is not sprayed over the hand that is holding the wooden form.

DYING THREAD, RIBBON AND FRINGING

- Tintex dyes by Australian Dye Manufacturers were used. Follow the instructions on the packets.

- Most of the fringing was dyed using hot water dye, to make it as colourfast as possible. This ensures that, when the tassel is resting against a curtain in humid weather, the dye will not run. (I live in Queensland, where the summer temperature is frequently over 35° C with 80% humidity.)

- As with all hand dyed products, it is recommended that they not be hung in strong, direct sunlight.

- For a two-tone effect, dip one end of the dampened fringing into one colour and the other end on the other colour. The colours will bleed in the middle.

Four Basic Steps

All the tassels in this book have been made using the following basic steps. Read these instructions carefully before you begin any of the projects. With each project you will also find specific notes to help you, and throughout the book further techniques are introduced to create variations of form and texture.

1. COVER THE WOODEN FORM

You will need a wooden form, thread and glue.

Using spray glue

You will need a rubber glove and some plastic wrap.

Cover the hips of the wooden form with plastic wrap, and put on a rubber glove to protect the hand that will be holding the tassel.

Spray two coats of glue over the wooden form, waiting two or three minutes between sprays so that the glue becomes quite tacky. After the second coat of glue, start winding the thread from the base of the wooden form, working slowly upward.

When you get to the top of the head, snip off the leftover thread leaving about ⅝ in (2 cm) hanging loose. Do not tuck in the loose end yet.

Using tacky craft glue

Starting from the bottom, apply a small amount of glue around the wooden form, then wind a few rows. Apply more glue, and wind a little further. Continue this procedure until you have finished the whole head.

When you get to the top of the head, snip off the leftover thread leaving about ⅘ in (2 cm) hanging loose. Do not tuck in the loose end yet.

Wrap the wooden form from the bottom to the top and leave a tail hanging loose at the top.

2. ATTACH THE SKIRT

Wrap the skirt (usually fringing) around the waist of the wooden form. Secure the ends of the skirt by stitching. Glue is not used for securing the skirt because it dries hard, making the fibres difficult to stitch through, and it is sometimes necessary to stitch through the top of the skirt when decorating the waist.

As the waists of the wooden forms vary slightly in size, determine how much fringing you will need by winding it around the waist several times before cutting the length. A trial wrap also helps you to control how thick the skirt will be. It seems that most tassel makers prefer a thicker skirt, so that it is not possible to see the wooden form through the skirt. However, it is a matter of personal taste, so, for those of you who prefer less fringing, this is the step to ensure you create the effect you want.

3. COVER THE WAIST

The waists of the tassels in this book are covered using either a ribbon or thread. If you are covering the waist with ribbon, simply join the ends of the ribbon with a needle and thread.

If you are covering the waist with thread, make a loop of thread and hold it against the waist, allowing the start of the thread to dangle free. Start wrapping upward from the bottom of the waist, covering the loop as you go but leaving the tip of the loop free. When you have finished wrapping, pass the end of the thread through the tip of the loop, and pull the start of the thread so that the end of the thread is drawn—by the loop—underneath the wrapping. Trim the start and the end of the thread so that they don't show.

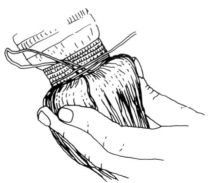

Make a loop, hold it against the waist and start wrapping.

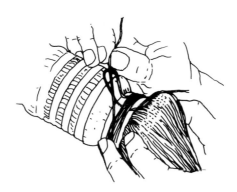

When you've finished wrapping the waist, pass the end of the thread through the loop and pull the loop under the wrapping.

4. ATTACH THE CORD

These instructions can be used with any type of cord or ribbon.

Fold the cord (or ribbon) in half. Tie the ends together with dental floss.

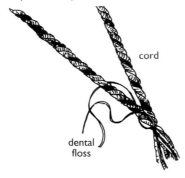

cord

dental
floss

Pass a wire through the folded end of the loop to make a 'threader'.

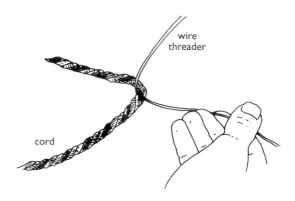

Pass the wire threader from the bottom of the wooden form through to the top.

Use the wire to pull the cord through the wooden form

Remove the threader wire, and pull the cord (or ribbon) through until the tied ends nearly reach the hole at the bottom of the form. Hook a shorter piece of wire through the tied end of the loop.

Pull the cord (or ribbon) through so that the knotted end of the cord disappears into the wooden form, but leave most of the short wire hanging out.

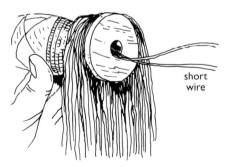

Twist the wire to prevent the cord (or ribbon) from being pulled through the hole in the wooden form.

Twisted wire stops the cord from slipping through the wooden form.

The Cord

MAKING YOUR OWN CORD

Plaiting can be used to make an effective three-coloured cord, and a simple twist can be used for making one- or two-coloured cord. Crocheting in chain stitch can make a one-coloured cord. You can also use any of the stunning ribbons available to make a simple matching hanging for your tassel. Experiment with the various possibilities, and choose your cord to match the colour and texture of your tassel.

Many of these projects specify handmade cord to match the threads on the tassel. Lengths of specific cording materials are given in each project, but any length of cord can be made to suit your personal taste, and any combination of threads and ribbons can be used.

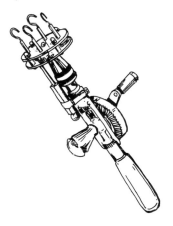

For the three- or four-stranded twists you will need a corder. Your local engineer can probably make you a corder; otherwise see the Suppliers at the back of this book.

A corder

stopper

USING A CORDER

First, the threads have to be twisted (with the stopper in the corder). Using the corder ensures that the threads all have the same number of twists so that they will fit together exactly to make the cord.

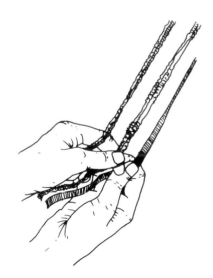

How to hold the threads when using a corder.

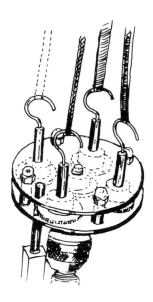

Loop the threads over the corder hooks.

With the corder stopper released, turn the handle to twist the threads together.

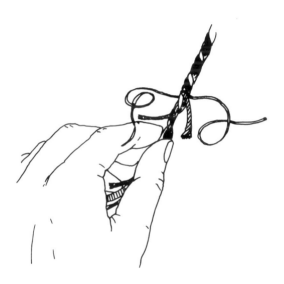

Tie the ends of the cord with dental floss to stop them unravelling.

The Head — Basic Wrapping

This project doesn't have a ruff or a skirt. It uses a wrapped wooden form and two wooden attachments to create a simple yet effective tassel.

Egg Tassel

REQUIREMENTS

Wooden form	*DC2 (includes the main wooden form and two attachments)*
Glue	*Spray glue*
Cord	*One packet of Kacoonda thick silk thread, colour 101*
Head	*One packet of Kacoonda thick silk thread, colour 101*

NOTES

- Carefully hold the main wooden form between your thumb and forefinger, covering as little of the ends as possible. Spray the form with glue and start wrapping from the base. At the top, leave a small piece of thread hanging to be tucked in after the cord.

- To make the cord, cut four 62 in (155 cm) lengths of the silk thread. Fold each one in half, and place them on the corder hooks. All four hooks of the corder will be used.

- To assemble the Egg Tassel: poke a wire through the tied ends of the cord and pull the wire and cord through the top attachment, then through the hole in the main wooden form. Remove the threader wire. Hook a shorter piece of wire through the bottom attachment and then through the tied end of the cord (see drawing). Pull the cord so that the wire disappears into the main wooden form.

Assembling the Egg Tassel.

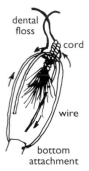

dental
floss

cord

wire

bottom
attachment

Detail of the wire securing the bottom attachment to the cord.

Simple Tassels with Ribbon Ruffs

The following three projects all use a simple ribbon ruff around the waist.

Small Tassel

This tassel is great for hanging from keys on cabinets and desks.

Requirements

Wooden form	*DC 102*
Glue	*Spray glue*
Cord	*Two 38 in (95 cm) lengths of chenille, colour blue jay (or any other matching colour)*
Head	*52 in (1.3 m) chenille, colour blue jay*
Ruff	*4 in (10 cm) Mokuba 4820, ⅜ in (10 mm) wide, colour 20*
Skirt	*10 in (25 cm) Birch Art 293903 fringing, white*

Notes

- You may wish to straighten the chenille by ironing it, but it is not necessary. The unironed chenille produces a lovely textured effect.

- Dye the fringing a colour to match the chenille thread and Mokuba ribbon.

- Make the cord using only two hooks on the corder.

$\mathcal{M}$ARABOUT THREAD TASSEL

This example uses an olive green and brown colour combination, but the marabout threads come in many different colours and lend themselves to a wide variety of combinations.

REQUIREMENTS

Wooden form	*Sullivans 48215*
Glue	*Spray glue*
Cord	*60 in (1.5 m) Mokuba 1505, ⅜ in (8 mm) wide, colour 26*
	3 x 60 in (3 x 1.5 m) Pebbly Perle, colour P54
	3 x 60 in (3 x 1.5 m) Neon Rays, colour N60
Head	*120 in (3 m) Marabout thread, colour mustard seed*
Ruff	*5 in (12.5 cm) Mokuba ribbon 4524, ⅝ in (15 mm) wide, colour 26*
Skirt	*Birch Art 293906 fringing, white*

NOTES

- Marabout thread has a right side and a wrong side. Depending on the final look you desire, you may like to iron the thread.

- Dye the fringing a colour to match your Marabout thread and Makuba ribbon.

- When making the cord, hook the Mokuba ribbon over one hook, the three strands of Pebbly Pearl over the second hook and the three strands of Neon Rays over the third hook.

$\mathcal{W}$AXED BRAID TASSEL

This tassel goes well with terracotta finishes so it looks good near indoor plants or in tiled rooms.

REQUIREMENTS

Wooden form	*Sullivans 48216*
Glue	*Tacky craft glue*
Cord	*64 in (1.6 m) Mokuba 570, colour 62*
	64 in (1.6 m) Mokuba 570, colour 33
Head	*84 in (2.1 m) Mokuba 570, colour 36*
	84 in (2.1 m) Mokuba 570, colour 62
	84 in (2.1 m) Mokuba 570, colour 33
Ruff	*15⅝ in (39 cm) ES1505, ⅜ in (12 mm) wide, colour 19*
Skirt	*Birch Art 293906 fringing, colour 76 (navy blue)*

NOTES

• To cover the head, wrap the three threads together, as if they are one. Hold them between your thumb and forefinger, making sure the colours don't twist around each other as you wind.

Simple Tassels with Wrapped-Thread Ruffs

R efer to the Four Basic Steps for how to wrap the waist using thread.

LITTLE RED TASSEL

This tassel is very easy and quite stunning.

REQUIREMENTS

Wooden form	*DC SP*
Glue	*Spray glue*
Cord	*Two 60 in (1.5 m) lengths of Pebbly Pearl 86*
	Two 60 in (1.5 m) lengths of the no. 3 cotton used for the head
Head	*Pearl no. 3 cotton, either a variegated colour or dyed to suit your taste*
Ruff	*Pebbly Pearl 86*
Skirt	*Birch Art 293906 fringing, colour 30 (red)*

NOTES

- To make the cord, use two of the hooks on the corder. Use the Pebbly Pearl on one hook and the cotton on the other hook.

$\mathcal{B}$ROWN BELL TASSEL

This is a very easy tassel to make. All that is required is the covering of the lower part of the bell and making the cord.

REQUIREMENTS

Wooden form	*DC 18*
Glue	*Spray glue*
Cord	*80 in (2 m) Mokuba 30, colour 14*
	Two 80 in (2 m) lengths of Mokuba 1504, ¹⁄₁₆ in (1.5 mm) wide, colour 45
	80 in (2 m) Mokuba 1505, ⅜ in (8 mm) wide, colour 43
Head	*Colour Streams Exotic Silk thread, colour 18*
Ruff	*16 in (4 m) Mokuba 1504, ¹⁄₁₆ in (1.5 mm) wide, colour 45 (brown)*
Skirt	*Birch Art 293906 fringing, colour 9*

NOTES

- Use the colour picture as a guide to changing threads as you wrap the wooden form.

- To make the cord, use four of the hooks on the corder, one thread per hook

$\mathcal{B}$RONZE METAL TASSEL

REQUIREMENTS

Wooden form	*DC 110*
Glue	*Spray glue or tacky craft glue*
Head	*Precious Metal, colour 3*
Ruff	*Precious Metal, colour 3*
Skirt	*Birch Art 293906 fringing, white*
Cord	*60 in (1.5 m) Precious Metal, colour 3*
	60 in (1.5 m) pearl cotton, colour black
	60 in (1.5 m) Mokuba 1512, colour black
	60 in (1.5 m) Mokuba 1540, ⅛ in (3.5 mm) wide, colour 600

NOTES

• Use the tacky craft glue if the spray glue won't hold the metallic thread.

• To make the cord, use four hooks on the corder, one thread per hook.

• Dye the fringing black.

Changing Colour when Wrapping the Wooden Form

As you wrap the wooden form, you can create interesting designs by changing the thread colour. Make sure that the ends of the threads are secured beneath the wrapping. For instance, if you are changing from purple to red, lay the red thread under the last few wraps of the purple. At the point where you want to change colour, cut the purple leaving a ¼ in (0.5 cm) tail. Start wrapping with the red, covering the purple tail as you go.

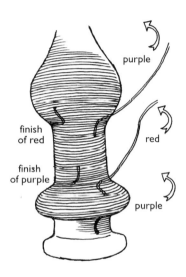

purple

finish
of red

red

finish
of purple

purple

Make sure the ends of each different colour are secured beneath the wrapping.

$\mathcal{S}$ILVER BELL TASSEL

REQUIREMENTS

Wooden form	*DC 16*
Glue	*Spray glue*
Cord	*Four 72 in (1.8 m) lengths of Cresta d'ora.*
Head	*Patina 82*
	Cresta d'ora 6 (silver)
Ruff	*Cresta d'ora 6 (silver)*
Skirt	*Birch Art 293906 fringing, white*

NOTES

- Use the colour picture as a guide to changing colours while wrapping the wooden form.

- Dye the fringing to match the threads. See Requirements for instructions on how to create the two-tone effect.

- To make the cord, use four hooks on the corder, one length of Cresta d'ora per hook.

$\mathcal{L}$ARGE LADY TASSEL

This tassel has a very easy cord. It is a commercially made one!

REQUIREMENTS

Wooden form	*DC 9*
Glue	*Spray glue*
Cord	*80 in (2 m) Birch 291305, colour 9*
Head	*Patina 245*
	Patina 240
	Patina 44
	Pearl no. 3 cotton
Ruff	*Patina (any colour that tones in with the pearl cotton)*
Skirt	*Birch Art 293912 fringing, colour 9*

NOTES

- Dye the Pearl no. 3 cotton a colour of your choice to match the other threads.

- Use the colour picture as a guide to changing colours while wrapping the wooden form.

$\mathscr{A}$RT DECO TASSEL

REQUIREMENTS

Wooden form	*DC 24*
Glue	*Spray glue*
Head	*27 ft (8 m) chenille (blue)*
	Pebbly Pearl 02 (white)
	Pebbly Pearl 19 (black)
	Mokuba 0934, colour 34 (gold)
Ruff	*7 in (18 cm) 4524 Mokuba, ⅝ in (15 mm) wide, colour 2 (white)*
	7 in (18 cm) 1505 Mokuba, ⅟₁₆ in (3.5 mm), colour 3 (black)
Skirt	*Birch Art 293912 fringing, colour 51 (gold)*
Cord	*Three 100 in (2.5 m) lengths of Birch 3061 (gold)*
	Two 100 in (2.5 m) lengths of Birch 003002 (white)

NOTES

• Use the colour picture as a guide to changing colours while wrapping the wooden form.

• To prepare the ribbon ruff, use black thread to stitch the black ribbon to the top of the white ribbon. Then attach the ruff in the usual way.

• To make the cord, use two hooks on the corder. Combine one length of white and two lengths of gold over one hook, and the remaining lengths of white and gold over the second hook.

$\mathcal{N}$AVY AND GOLD TASSEL

This is an elegant tassel. It would look great simply hanging from a hook on the wall or hooked over the back of dining room chairs.

REQUIREMENTS

Wooden form	*DC 13*
Glue	*Spray glue*
Cord	*Four 80 in (2 m) lengths of Mokuba 1512, colour 19 (navy blue)*
	Three 80 in (2 m) lengths of Mokuba 0959, colour 14 (gold)
Head	*23 ft (7 m) Mokuba 0959 thin cord, colour 19 (navy blue)*
	50 ft (15 m) Mokuba 0959 thin cord, colour 14 (gold)
Ruff	*7 in (17.5 cm) Mokuba ribbon 4564, ⅛ in (5 mm) wide, colour 14*
Skirt	*Birch Art 293912 fringing, colour 76 (navy blue)*

NOTES

- Use the colour picture as a guide to changing colours while wrapping the wooden form.

- To make the cord, hook the navy blue ribbon over one hook and the gold cord over the other hook.

Decorating the Head

A ny decoration can be used to embellish the head. Here are two projects that use thread and decorative ribbon.

Olive top tassel with flowers

Requirements

Wooden form	*Sullivans 48216*
Glue	*Spray glue*
Cord	*Six 64 in (1.6 m) lengths of Pebbly Pearl 76*
Head	*Pebbly Pearl 76*
	24 in (60 cm) Mokuba flower braid 9317, colour 5
Ruff	*20 in (50 cm) Mokuba flower braid 9317, colour 5*
Skirt	*Birch Art 293906 fringing, colour 51 (gold)*

Notes

- To wrap the flower braid around the head, daub a bit of glue on the back of a flower with a toothpick. Position the flower on the head and hold it in place for a few seconds.

- Make the cord using three hooks on the corder, two lengths of Pebbly Pearl per hook.

$\mathcal{G}$REEN AND BROWN TASSEL

REQUIREMENTS

Wooden form	*DC 51*
Glue	*Spray glue*
	Craft glue
Cord	*160 in (4 m) Mokuba 1504, colour 45*
	80 in (2 m) Mokuba 30, colour 14
Head	*Kacoonda thick silk 8B*
	Kacoonda thick silk 6C
	40 in (1 m) Mokuba braid 0843, colour 14
Ruff	*80 in (2 m) Mokuba braid 0843, colour 14*
Skirt	*Birch Art 293906 fringing, white*

NOTES

• Dye the fringing a colour of your choice to match the threads.

• The braid is glued on, after covering the wooden form, using tacky craft glue and a toothpick. Dip the toothpick in the glue and wipe it onto the back of the braid. Carefully lay the braid in place, and hold it down for a few seconds until the glue is dry.

• To make the cord, use three hooks on the corder. Place the fine ribbon over one hook and the brown cord over the other two hooks.

The Skirt — Decorating a Fringe Skirt
MINISKIRT TASSEL

REQUIREMENTS

Wooden form	*DC 51*
Glue	*Spray glue*
Cord	*160 in (4 m) Mokuba 1540, colour 360*
	80 in (2 m) apricot ribbon floss
	160 in (4 m) Pebbly Pearl, colour 74
	80 in (2 m) Mokuba organdy #1500, ⅛ in (5 mm) width, colour 44
Head	*One packet of Kacoonda thick silk 6F*
	Patina 81
Ruff	*Pebbly Pearl 74*
Skirt	*Birch Art 293906 fringing, white*
	About 5½ in (14 cm) Birch Art 287245 fringing, white

NOTES

- Iron the Patina 81 rayon thread.

- The rayon and the silk threads are wound around the wooden form simultaneously.

- Dye the fringing two complementary colours, to match the other threads.

- Wrap the 6 in (15 cm) skirt around the waist and stitch down the end. Then wrap the short fringing over the top and stitch the end.

$\mathcal{P}$URPLE TASSEL

REQUIREMENTS

Wooden form	*DC 14*
Glue	*Spray glue*
Cord	*Two 64 in (1.6 m) lengths of purple chenille*
	Any gold thread for highlights
Head	*Colour Streams Exotic silk thread 14*
Ruff	*80 in (2 m) chenille, purple*
Skirt	*Birch Art 293906 fringing, white (dyed violet)*
	Colour Streams ¼ in (7 mm) silk ribbon, colour 14

NOTES

- Use the colour picture as a guide to changing colours while wrapping the wooden form.

- After attaching the violet fringing, hang loops of ribbon around the outside of the skirt at six, evenly spaced intervals. Then wrap the chenille around the waist.

$\mathcal{P}$URPLE AND RED TASSEL

REQUIREMENTS

Wooden form	*DC 25*
Glue	*Spray glue*
Cord	*Anchor pearl cotton 8, colour 47 (red)*
Head	*Anchor pearl cotton 8, colour 47 (red)*
	Patina 267
Ruff	*Two 7 m corded lengths of Anchor pearl cotton 8, colour 47 (red)*
Skirt	*Birch Art 293906 fringing, white (dyed violet)*
	18 in (45 cm) Plummets (fiesta)

NOTES

* Iron the creases out of the Patina 267.

* Cut two 15 ½ yard (14 m) lengths of the Anchor pearl cotton. Twist the lengths together to make a fine cord for wrapping the wooden form.

* Use the colour picture as a guide to changing colours while wrapping the wooden form.

* Wrap the skirt around the waist and stitch down the end of the fringing. Then stitch the plummets onto the waist.

* To make the cord: first twist the rest of the roll of Anchor pearl cotton; then hook 80 in (2 m) lengths of the corded red cotton over each hook.

Ribbon Skirts

Ribbon skirts are the ultimate in designer tassels!

HOW TO MAKE A RIBBON SKIRT

1. Cut a piece of cardboard to the required size. One side of the cardboard rectangle is the length of the fringing; the other side is a few centimetres longer than the measurement around the waist.

2. Thread a needle and cotton. Make the thread double and tie a knot in the end.

3. Hold a thin skewer (a satay stick or knitting needle is ideal) along the waist measurement length of the cardboard. The skewer is used to hold the ribbon slightly above the cardboard to create a space in which to sew the ribbon loops together.

4. Wind the ribbon once around the cardboard and skewer.

5. Do a couple of small backstitches to secure the ribbon loop. Continue in this way: wind around, do backstitches, wind around and do backstitches.

Hold the thin skewer along the top of the card as you wrap the ribbon.

$\mathcal{H}$AND DYED RIBBON WITH WOODEN TOP

REQUIREMENTS

Wooden form	*DC 1*
Glue	*Tacky craft glue*
Cord	*Patina to match the dyed two strands per hook*
Skirt	*Makuba ribbon no. 1512, white (dyed)*
	Makuba ribbon, two other solid colours to match

NOTES

- Make the cord first and insert it through the centre of the form.

- Make the ribbon skirt, then roll it up along the stitched edge, so that the top of the skirt can be pushed into the hole in the bottom of the wooden form.

- Using your finger, apply some glue to the top of the skirt roll, then apply some more glue inside the hole in the bottom of the wooden form. Position the coiled skirt in the hole.

- Dry the tassel resting horizontally—not hanging vertically—so that the skirt doesn't fall out.

$\mathcal{G}$REEN RIBBON TASSEL

REQUIREMENTS

Wooden form	*DC 14*
Glue	*Spray glue and tacky craft glue*
Cord	*Three 80 in (2 m) lengths of Mokuba 0934, colour 74 (bronze)*
	Three 80 in (2 m) lengths of either colour of Patina
Head	*80 in (2 m) Mokuba 0934, colour 74*
	Patina 251
	Patina 261
Ruff	*80 in (2 m) Mokuba 0934, colour 74*
Skirt	*33 yd (30 m) Mokuba ES1540, ⅜ in (7 mm) wide, colour 366*

NOTES

- Iron the Patina thread to remove creases.

- Use the colour picture as a guide to changing colours while wrapping the wooden form.

- Make the ribbon fringe in two layers. The first layer of ribbon uses 22 yd (20 m) and each wrap is done four times before backstitching. The second layer uses 11 yd (10 m) and has two wraps before backstitching.

- Join the skirt to the wooden form using tacky craft glue.

- To make the cord, hook the bronze thread over one hook and the Patina over the other hook.

$\mathscr{P}$ASTEL RIBBON TASSEL

REQUIREMENTS

Wooden form	*Sullivans 48216*
Glue	*Spray glue*
Cord	*64 in (1.6 m) Mokuba 1543, ⅜ in (7 mm) wide, variegation colour 8*
	64 in (1.6 m) Mokuba 0925, colour 31
Head	*11 yd (10 m) Mokuba 0925, colour 31*
Ruff	*5⅛ in (13 cm) Birch double satin ribbon 001163, ⅜ in (10 mm) wide, colour yellow 679*
	12 in (30 cm) Mokuba flower braid 9317, colour 4
Skirt	*33 yd (30 m) Mokuba 1543, ⅜ in (7 mm), colour 8*

NOTES

- Make the ribbon fringe in two layers. The first layer requires the ribbon to be wound four times before backstitching, and the second layer has two wraps before backstitching.

- Wrap the waist with the yellow ribbon before stitching the flower braid over the top.

REQUIREMENTS

Wooden form	*DC 110*
Glue	*Tacky craft glue*
Cord	*60 in (1.5 m) Mokuba 0925, colour 15 (goldish colour)*
	Two 5 ft (1.5 m) lengths of Mokuba 0925, colour 31 (pink)
	60 in (1.5 m) Mokuba 1500 organdy ribbon, ¼ in (5 mm) wide, colour 31
Head	*104 in (2.6 m) Mokuba jewellery yarn 0150, colour 31*
Ruff	*80 in (2 m) Mokuba 0925, colour 15 (goldish colour)*
Skirt	*50 yd (45 m) Mokuba 1500 organdy ribbon, ¼ in (5 mm) wide, colour 31*

NOTES

- This fringe is done in two layers. The first layer has the ribbon wound around three times before backstitching, and the second layer has the wound around twice before backstitching.

- Three of the hooks on the corder are used, one for each colour.

The Ruff — Decorating the Waist
Turquoise METAL TASSEL

REQUIREMENTS

Wooden form	*Sullivans 48218*
Glue	*Tacky craft glue*
Cord	*80 in (2 m) Kreinik 018 heavy #32 braid*
	80 in (2 m) Kreinik 52HL heavy #32 braid
	Two 80 in (2 m) lengths of Mokuba 0925 teal gimp, colour 46
	80 in (2 m) Mokuba 1546 (7 mm wide) ribbon, colour 317
Head	*90 in (2.25 m) Kreinik 52HL heavy #32 braid*
	90 in (2.25 m) Kreinik 018 heavy #32 braid
	Two 90 in (2.25 m) lengths of Mokuba 0925 teal gimp, colour 46
Ruff	*6¼ in (17 cm) Mokuba 4524, ⅝ in (15 mm) wide, colour 7*
	Mill Hill antique glass beads #03036
Skirt	*Birch Art 293912 fringing, white*

NOTES

- Four strands of thread are wound around the wooden form simultaneously. The order is blue-coloured metal, gimp, gimp then brown-coloured metal.

- Sew the beads on the non-velvet squares of the ribbon ruff before wrapping it around the waist.

- To make the cord, hook the ribbon over one hook, the blue metal over another, the brown metal thread over another, and two lengths of gimp over the last hook.

𝒯URKISH DELIGHT TASSEL

REQUIREMENTS

Wooden form	*Sullivans 48216*
Glue	*Spray glue and tacky craft glue*
Cord	*Colour Streams Exotic Silk, colour 14*
	Rayon thread, (dyed) twisted into a fine cord
Head	*Colour Streams Exotic Silk, colour 14*
	Rayon thread (dyed), twisted corded into a fine cord
Ruff	*⅛ in (7 mm) variegated silk ribbon*
Skirt	*Three harmonious colours of fringing. In this case, a core of turquoise is covered by a layer of purple and an outer layer of navy blue.*

NOTES

- Make the cord using four hooks on the corder. Loop one strand of twisted cord each on two of the hooks and three strands of exotic silk on the two remaining hooks.

- The silk and the corded rayon are wrapped around the wooden form simultaneously.

- Make the ribbon ruff as follows. With tailor's chalk measure the ribbon every 3 in (7.5 cm) to mark the folds at the top and the bottom of the decoration. Stitch the ribbon together as you fold. Then stitch the ribbon to the waist of the tassel, making sure you completely cover the woven top of the fringing.

Gathered-Ribbon Ruffs

The following two tassels have gathered-ribbon ruffs. This technique can be used on any tassel to add texture and colour.

The ruffles are sewn on after the fringing has been attached to the waist. Secure the end of the ribbon to the top of the fringing. Then gather a small amount of the ribbon on the needle to form a ruffle. Stitch the ruffle to the top of the fringing. Repeat the process—gathering and stitching as you go—until the waist is covered with ruffles.

Straight stitch along the ribbon without pulling the needle through.

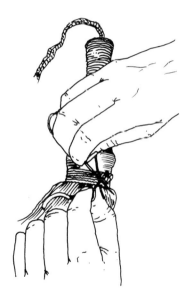

Gather the ribbon on the needle.

Secure the gathered ribbon to the top of the fringing.

$\mathscr{P}$INK TASSEL WITH YELLOW SKIRT

REQUIREMENTS

Wooden form	*Sullivans 48216*
Glue	*Spray glue*
Cord	*64 in (1.6 m) Mokuba 1543, ⅛ in (7 mm) wide, variegation colour 8*
	64 in (1.6 m) Mokuba 0925, colour 31
Head	*11 yd (10 m) Mokuba 0925, colour 31*
Ruff	*5 ft (1.5 m) Mokuba 1543, colour 8*
Skirt	*Birch Art 293906 fringing, white (dyed yellow)*
	20 in (50 cm) Mokuba flower braid 9317, colours 4 and 6

NOTES

- Cut the flower braid in the middle of the green sections. Fold the ends back to form leaf-like edges, and stitch the ends behind the flower. Attach the flowers to the fringing, going from darker flowers at the bottom of the skirt to lighter flowers at the top.

Snip the flower braid between the flowers.

Fold back the ends, and stitch them behind the flower.

$\mathcal{P}$RETTY LIGHT-PINK TASSEL

REQUIREMENTS

Wooden form	*Sullivans 48215*
Glue	*Spray glue*
Cord	*Two 64 in (1.6 m) lengths of Pebbly Pearl 11*
	Four 64 in (1.6 m) Colour Streams Exotic Silk, colour 12
Head	*Colour Streams Exotic Silk, colour 12*
Ruff	*Colour Streams, ⅜ in (7 mm) wide, silk ribbon, colour 12*
Skirt	*Birch Art 293906 fringing, colour pink*
	Colour Streams, ⅜ in (7 mm) wide, silk ribbon, colour 12

NOTES

- Wrap the skirt around the waist and stitch the end of the fringing. Sew six, evenly spaced loops of silk ribbon onto the top of the fringing. Then sew the gathered ribbon ruff over the top.

Soft Tassels

To make a soft tassel, first cut a piece of card 2 in (5 cm) deep. Wind a double strand of thread ten times around the card to form the body of the tassel. Slip a thread through the top of the loops to tie them together and to form a shank for the tassel to hang from. Remove the tassel from the card, then wrap a double thread three times around the tassel (near the top) to make a soft 'head'. Cut the bottoms of the loops.

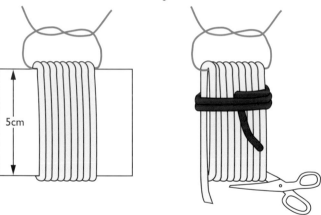

Wind the double thread around 2 in (5 cm) card. Slip a thread through the top to form a shank. Remove the card and wrap thread around the loops to form a 'head'. Then snip the bottoms of the loops.

$\mathcal{B}$RIAR ROSE TASSEL

REQUIREMENTS

Wooden form	*Sullivans 48215*
Glue	*Spray glue and tacky craft glue*
Cord	*40 in (1 m) Mokuba ribbon 4881, 1½ in (38 mm) wide, colour 2*
Head	*Viscose gimp (dyed)*
Ruff	*80 in (2 m) Mokuba ribbon 4881, 3 in (75 mm) wide, colour 2*
Skirt	*28 in (70 cm) Birch Art 293906, white (dyed pink)*
	Gumnut Yarns Buds Silk, colour 851 (for the soft tassels)

NOTES

- Use tacky craft glue with the viscose gimp.

- Make eight soft tassels out of the GYB 851 with shanks about 6 in (15 cm) long. After the fringing has been secured to the waist, stitch the tassels to the top of the fringing at evenly spaced intervals.

- The ribbon roses are attached to the waist after the soft tassels. Each rose is formed using approximately 5⅛ in (13 cm) of ribbon. Loosely tie the first step of a granny knot, arranging the folds to simulate a 'full blown' rose. Secure the roses with a few tiny stitches to the top of the fringing. The ribbon ends can be trimmed if necessary then tucked under the flower shape. Sew small French knots in the centre of each rose using two strands of stranded cotton.

Form the ribbon roses by tying a loose knot.

Suppliers

THREADS & MORE
32 Couldrey Street
Bardon Q 4065
AUSTRALIA
Tel: +61 (07) 3371 5835
Fax: +61 (07) 3371 5835
Email: threadsmore@uq.net.au

The following items can be mailed ordered or purchased from Threads & More:

> Tassels in kits
> Wooden forms
> Hand and commercially dyed threads
> Dyed fringing
> Novelty threads and yarns
> Coloured canvas
> Ribbons
> Colour Stream, Gumnut, Kaalund, Kacoonda, and Rainbow Gallery threads

Threads & More also offers a finishing service.

Some of the equipment, ribbons and threads used in this book can also be purchased from the following retail outlets. If they do not carry the exact thread, these shops will be able to provide very close substitutes. They all provide excellent service and will mail any requirements anywhere.

ANNA CRUTCHLEY
The Frater Studio
6b Priory Road
Cambridge CB5 8HT
UNITED KINGDOM
Phone: +44 (01223) 327685
Wooden forms and corders

AUSTRALIAN DYE MANUFACTURERS
240 South Pine Road
Enoggera Qld 4051
AUSTRALIA
Ph: +61 (07) 3855 2801
Wholesale dyes

DOWN UNDER AUSTRALIA
PO Box 9
Seaforth NSW 2092
AUSTRALIA
Ph: +61 (02) 9948 5575
Fax: +61 (02) 9948 7172
Wholesale only: Patina, Neon Rays and Pebbly Pearl, Precious Metal threads.

E. C. BIRCH PTY LTD
36–50 Robertson Street
Fortitude Valley Qld 4006
AUSTRALIA
Ph: +61 (07) 3252 5205
Fax: +61 (07) 3252 4999
Freecall (Australia only): 1-800 773
010
Wholesale: Fringing

KAY PYKE
359 Bay Street
Port Melbourne Vic 3207
AUSTRALIA
Ph: +61 (03) 9646 3540

MILLER & COATS
Shop 8 Ascot Village
Cnr Lancaster and Racecourse Roads
Ascot Qld 4007
AUSTRALIA
Ph: +61 (07) 3268 3955

PACIFIC FAIR HANDCRAFTS
Shop 195 Pacific Fair Shopping
Centre
Broadbeach Qld 4218
AUSTRALIA

SULLIVANS
40 Parramatta Road
Underwood Qld 4119
AUSTRALIA
Ph: +61 (07) 3209 4799
Fax: +61 (07) 3208 9410
Freecall (Australia only): 1-800 777
582
Wholesale: wooden forms

ACKNOWLEDGMENTS

I would like to thank the children of Couldrey Street—Carolyn and Richard Gibbs, Catriona and Alexander Rose—for the many hours they have spent helping me set up for such a project.

Many thanks also go to Glenda Andrews, Kay Conway, Margaret Dyne, Bev Folliott, Noel Hill and Barbara Timmons for so willingly and generously sharing their valuable time and expertise with me for the duration of this project.